Summary of

The Immortal Irishman

by Timothy Egan

Instaread

Please Note

This is a summary with analysis.

Table of Contents

Overview 4

Important People 8

Key Takeaways...10

Analysis 12

Key Takeaway 1 12

Key Takeaway 2 14

Key Takeaway 3 16

Key Takeaway 4 17

Key Takeaway 5 19

Key Takeaway 6 21

Key Takeaway 7 23

Key Takeaway 8 25

Author's Style 27

Author's Perspective 28

References 30

Overview

Timothy Egan's *The Immortal Irishman* is a biography of Thomas Meagher: Irish revolutionary, convict, and Civil War general. The book also offers a broad portrait of the experiences of the Irish during the period, both at home and abroad.

Meagher was born in 1823 into a prominent and wealthy Catholic family. This gave him advantages of education and standing. At the same time, Catholics in Ireland were brutally oppressed, with limits on landholding, political representation, and religion. Meagher was an outspoken opponent of British oppression and British rule, and became known for his stirring and fiery oratory.

Meagher became even more radicalized by the Irish Potato Famine that began in 1845. The famine was caused by a potato blight which destroyed half or more of the crop in Ireland for a number of years. The famine was exacerbated by British refusal to provide aid to the Irish.

Meagher joined with the radical group Young Ireland in calling for violent resistance to British rule.

He participated in an abortive uprising in 1848, after which he was imprisoned. He and other Young Ireland leaders were exiled to Van Diemen's Land, or Tasmania, Australia. He left Ireland in 1849, never to see his homeland again.

Meagher was in Australia for two years. He promised not to try to escape and so had limited freedom of movement. In 1851, he married Catherine Bennett, the daughter of a transported convict, much to the dismay of his fellow political prisoners. Shortly thereafter, in 1852, he renounced his promise not to escape and fled with prearranged help to the United States. His wife, who was pregnant, stayed behind and bore a son who lived only a few months. Catherine later went to Ireland to join Meagher's father.

During and after the famine, hundreds of thousands of Irish people emigrated. Many of them went to the United States, especially to port cities such as New York, where Meagher settled. He was received as a hero by the Irish community for his role in the Young Ireland rebellion, and he began to make a living as a speaker. His wife joined him briefly but then returned to Ireland. She died in childbirth in 1854 after giving birth to a son. Meagher, banned from Ireland, was never to see his child. He soon remarried, this time to Elizabeth Townsend, a wealthy Protestant who converted to Catholicism before they were wed.

Meagher initially felt it would be damaging to the Union to abolish slavery and therefore had some sympathy for the South. Like many Irish, he worried that free blacks would compete with Irish Americans for jobs. However, after the attack on Fort Sumter, Meagher saw the South as aggressors and decided to fight for the Union. He helped recruit Irish men in New York. He eventually became brigadier general of the Irish Brigade, also known as the 69th Brigade.

Meagher and his brigade fought at the First Battle of Bull Run in 1861 and took terrible losses at the Battle of Antietam in 1862. The unit was decimated at the Battle of Fredericksburg at the end of that year. Meagher, who suffered from an ulcer on his knee, retired his commission soon afterwards.

The losses in the war and his controversial support for the Union caused Meagher's reputation to take a beating in the Irish American community. Violent riots against the military draft in New York in 1863 demonstrated the extent of Irish opposition to the war and to the emancipation of slaves. Nonetheless, Meagher campaigned for Abraham Lincoln's reelection in 1864.

After the Union victory in 1865, Meagher was appointed acting governor of the Montana Territory. His presence and his sympathy for the Democratic Party angered Republicans. Many Republican leaders in Montana were involved in vigilante murders of criminals and those who crossed them. Meagher's difficulties were compounded by the fact that the federal government did not send him his promised salary.

Broke and frustrated, Meagher was preparing to leave the territories. However, on a trip on business on the

Missouri River, he fell overboard and died. His body was never recovered. Some suggested Meagher had fallen by accident or because he was drunk. Wilbur Sanders, one of Meagher's Republican enemies, even said that Meagher may have committed suicide. However, there is suggestive evidence that Meagher was murdered and that it was arranged by his political opponents, including Sanders himself.

Meagher is remembered today by the Irish and Irish Americans as a patriot and a war hero.

Important People

Timothy Egan is a journalist known for his works of popular history. In addition to *The Immortal Irishman*, other books include *The Worst Hard Time: The Untold Story of Those Who Survived the Great American Dust Bowl* (2005) and *The Big Burn: Teddy Roosevelt and the Fire That Saved America* (2009).

Thomas Francis Meagher (1823-1867) was an Irish nationalist who opposed British rule. After being transported to Australia by the British, he escaped to the United States where he fought for the Union army in the Civil War.

Thomas Meagher (1796-1874) was Thomas Francis Meagher's father. He was a successful Catholic businessman in Ireland and became a member of Parliament.

Jane Elgee (1821-1896) was a supporter of Young Ireland who wrote anti-British and Irish nationalist poetry under the name Speranza. She may have been Thomas Meagher's lover. She later married Sir William Wilde and was the mother of the famous poet and dramatist Oscar Wilde.

William Smith O'Brien (1803-1864) was a leader of the Young Ireland movement and a member of Parliament. He was deported to Van Diemen's Land along with Meagher.

John Mitchel (1815-1875) was an Irish nationalist, a writer, and a leader of Young Ireland. After being transported from Ireland, he eventually escaped to America where he became an advocate for slavery and the Confederacy.

Catherine Bennett "Bennie" Meagher (1832?-1854) was Thomas Meagher's first wife. She was born in Australia to a transported convict. She and Meagher had two sons, one who died in infancy. She died giving birth to the second, also named Thomas, who was born in Ireland.

George B. McClellan (1826-1885) was the leader of the Union forces during the early part of the Civil War. He respected the Irish Brigade and was a great favorite with its members, who were devastated when he was removed as commander in 1862.

Elizabeth Townsend Meagher (1830-1906) was the daughter of a wealthy Protestant New York family. Despite her parents' disapproval, she converted to Catholicism and married Thomas Meagher in 1855.

Ambrose Burnside (1824-1881) was a Union army commander during the Civil War. He was in command at the Battle of Antietam and the Battle of Fredericksburg, during both of which the Irish Brigade sustained severe losses.

Wilbur Sanders (1834-1905) was a Republican political leader in the Montana Territory. He was one of Meagher's political enemies and may have been involved in his death.

Key Takeaways

1. British imperial control exacerbated the Irish Potato Famine and led to hundreds of thousands of deaths.

2. Young Ireland, a pro-Irish independence group, vacillated in advocating violence against British rule.

3. Britain used transportation as a punishment for both criminals and political prisoners.

4. Van Diemen's Land and Ireland illustrate Britain's inconsistent imperial policy. Van Diemen's Land was granted the independence that Ireland was long denied.

5. Massive waves of immigration to the United States from Ireland after the potato famine provoked an anti-immigrant backlash.

6. The Irish in America were often pro-slavery. Meagher's support for the Union was therefore controversial in his community.

7. The Irish Brigade fought valiantly for the Union in the Civil War.

8. The Montana Territory was plagued by vigilante justice. The violence may have led to Meagher's death.

Thank you for purchasing this Instaread book

**Download the Instaread mobile app to get
unlimited text & audio summaries
of bestselling books.**

Visit Instaread.co
to learn more.

Analysis

Key Takeaway 1

British imperial control exacerbated the Irish Potato Famine and led to hundreds of thousands of deaths.

Analysis

The potato blight, which first appeared in Ireland in 1845, destroyed the staple crop of the poor. Half of the planted potatoes were blighted in that year, and even more were ruined in the following seasons. Hundreds of thousands of Irish peasants starved.

Rather than providing meaningful aid, the British authorities affirmed their belief in free trade and refused to interfere with markets. The British shipped more than a billion pounds of grain out of Ireland for export in 1845 even as people starved. The massive suffering of the Irish people helped fuel the nationalist Young Ireland movement, which demanded Irish independence.

In the years since the famine, historians have largely agreed that British policy decisions made the situation worse. The exact degree of British responsibility, though, has been a matter of dispute. In his 2012 book *The Graves Are Walking*, John Kelly places the blame for the famine on misguided British ideology. The British saw the famine as an opportunity to modernize Ireland and this was more important to them than saving lives. So the British created a public works scheme in which laborers were hired to build roads, which were unneeded, in order to have an excuse to pay wages and shift Ireland from a barter economy towards the use of money. Even with their wages, though, laborers often couldn't afford food. [1]

Kelly regards these actions as British negligence, abetted by prejudice and ignorance. Tim Pat Coogan's *The Famine Plot*, also from 2012, arrives at even harsher conclusions. Coogan describes the British policy as genocide. He points out that the British hated the Irish and often blamed the famine on Irish immorality or backwardness. British tabloids portrayed the Irish as apes. The loathing of the Irish, Coogan argues, led to a policy designed to let the people starve. Racial hatred leading to mass death, he concludes, constituted genocide. [2]

Key Takeaway 2

Young Ireland, a pro-Irish independence group, vacillated in advocating violence against British rule.

Analysis

Daniel O'Connell, the great Irish leader who had led the successful mass movement for Catholic emancipation in 1829, was committed to nonviolent tactics. The Young Ireland movement, including Meagher, more explicitly called for revolution and for violent resistance to British rule.

When Meagher was arrested at home, however, he did not call for revolution. Thousands of Irish supporters, eager to engage the police, surrounded his home. Meagher asked them to remain calm. The British had better weapons and trained troops. Meagher was militant, but he did not want to see Irish people die.

Peaceful demonstrations did not move Britain to provide aid, but armed uprising was practically impossible. Young Ireland's 1848 Revolution was tiny and was quickly and ignominiously put down. However, it became an inspiration for later protest movements, which moved away from O'Connell's nonviolence and toward more open rejection of the constitutional system in favor of rebellion, often using violent means.

The suppressed rebellion of 1916 was indebted to the Young Ireland movement, as was the rebellion which resulted in Irish independence in 1921 and the separation of Northern Ireland, which remained part of the United Kingdom. Young Ireland also helped to inspire the long campaign of terrorist violence launched by Sinn Féin against Britain into the 1990s, whose objectives were to give the Irish government control over the entire island. [3]

In addition to its violent legacy, however, Young Ireland left an important peaceful legacy. The nationalist writing and poetry of the group was widely distributed. The paper of Young Ireland, *The Nation*, used the tagline "Educate that you may be free." Young Irelanders also established a publishing imprint, the Library of Ireland, which put out a series of books on important moments in Irish history. The Library of Ireland also released popular ballads, which framed Ireland's history in terms of glory and struggle. So while Young Ireland advocated the sword, the bulk of their work involved the pen, through which they inculcated the spirit of Irish nationalism which, after decades, finally led to Irish independence. [4]

Key Takeaway 3

Britain used transportation as a punishment for both criminals and political prisoners.

Analysis

Britain in the 1800s regularly sent prisoners to Australia. Transportation began in 1788. [5] Most prisoners were transported for crimes like small-scale theft or avoiding rent payments. Only a very small number of those sent to Australia were political prisoners like the Young Irelanders.

After good behavior, convicts could be released on a ticket of leave, at which point they could live independently, though convicts could be taken back into custody for infractions. Originally tickets of leave were intended to save money, because convicts working on their own did not have to be fed or housed by the authorities. Tickets of leave also turned out to be a good way to enforce discipline. Prisoners were willing to obey orders when they had the chance of being released with a ticket of leave. [6]

Key Takeaway 4

Van Diemen's Land and Ireland illustrate Britain's inconsistent imperial policy. Van Diemen's Land was granted the independence that Ireland was long denied.

Analysis

Ireland was conquered by Britain in 1171. It became the first of Britain's empire of colonies, and in many ways the most difficult to control. At first, Britain allowed Ireland its own Parliament but abolished it in 1801. Young Ireland was, in part, committed to re-establishing an Irish Parliament. In contrast, Van Diemen's Land was granted increasing legislative self-government, culminating in independence in 1856, without revolution.

Though the British were in some ways more lenient towards Van Diemen's Land than towards Ireland, the colony also experienced the same kind of imperial brutality that Ireland experienced during the famine. The British arrived in Tasmania in 1803, but there was little colonial settlement for the next two decades. As the white population grew, however, there was more and more conflict with the native Tasmanian people. During the battles that followed, the colonists experienced significant losses, but the indigenous people were eventually all but exterminated. [7] In part, this was because of disease, but colonists also killed Tasmanians in order to take their land. More than 800 Tasmanians were killed during these battles with the colonists. [8]

The destruction of the Tasmanian people became the inspiration for H.G. Wells's famous *War of the Worlds*, in which Martians invade England. As he tried to understand the Martian invasion, the narrator of *War of the Worlds* compared the destruction of England to the destruction of Tasmania. "The Tasmanians, in spite of their human likeness, were entirely swept out of existence in a war of extermination waged by European immigrants, in the space of fifty years," the narrator says. [9] Wells does not mention the Irish, but they too, perhaps, saw the British as invaders sweeping in to plunder, pillage, and kill.

Key Takeaway 5

Massive waves of immigration to the United States from Ireland after the potato famine provoked an anti-immigrant backlash.

Analysis

When Thomas Meagher arrived in New York City after escaping from Van Diemen's Land, he found many of his countrymen waiting for him. In an effort to escape the famine, almost 850,000 Irish people immigrated to the United States between 1847 and 1851. There they lived in crowded and unsanitary conditions, but they also enjoyed freedoms they never had in Ireland. They could practice their religion without harassment, and they could speak against Britain without fear of reprisal.

The Irish did face prejudice, even in America. A nativist political faction, the Know-Nothings, opposed Catholic immigration and attempted to pass legislation preventing Irish and other Catholics from becoming citizens. The Know-Nothings never gained much influence on the federal level, nor did they manage to win many victories in New York City. However, they did take control of a number of state governments. Their biggest triumph occurred in 1854, when the American Party, the official Know-Nothing party apparatus, captured the governorship and legislature of Massachusetts. Once in power, the American Party passed a raft of anti-immigration and nativist measures. In a wantonly cruel act, the Massachusetts government sent 300 poor and mentally ill

Irish wards of the state to Liverpool, without making provisions for their care. [10]

Finally, the Know-Nothings instituted strict restrictions on alcohol sales. Alcohol was stereotypically understood to be a particularly Irish and Catholic vice, but restricting it proved very unpopular with people of every religion. The party was further damaged by the issue of slavery, which divided many of its voters. The American Party lost control of the Massachusetts government in 1860 when many of its voters bolted for the anti-slavery Republican Party. [11]

Though there is no longer widespread discrimination against Irish Americans, anti-immigrant sentiment has remained a strong force in US politics. For example, in 2016, anti-immigrant rhetoric directed at Mexicans and Muslims fueled the presidential campaign of Donald Trump.

Key Takeaway 6

The Irish in America were often pro-slavery. Meagher's support for the Union was therefore controversial in his community.

Analysis

In Ireland, Irish people had experienced grinding prejudice and oppression. When they came to the United States, many sympathized with the plight of the slaves and argued for their freedom. Others, however, saw slaves as competition and worried that freed slaves might take good jobs from Irish laborers. Many Irish also were prejudiced against black people.

Meagher himself was against freeing the slaves but supported the Union. He was joined by many others in the Irish community. The Emancipation Proclamation, which freed the slaves, eroded support for the war among many Irish people, as did heavy losses in Meagher's Irish Brigade.

In part because of such tensions, many Irish people participated in the 1863 riots in New York City against the draft, in which over a hundred people were killed, black people were assaulted, and many African Americans were forced to leave the city to escape the mobs. Meagher himself, however, continued to support Lincoln and the Union throughout the war.

Racism was not confined to the Irish; many white Northerners of every ethnicity held racist views. Free blacks in the North were often harassed or even driven out of towns by white people. Many working-class whites, like the Irish, saw black people as potential competition for jobs. [12]

There were some abolitionists who believed in the equality of black people and who saw the end of slavery as a moral imperative. Most Northern whites, however, wanted the United States to remain united and feared Southern dominance, but had little wish to free the slaves. This opinion changed to some extent during the course of the war, especially as black soldiers fought bravely for the Union. But even at the time of the Emancipation Proclamation in 1863, many Northern whites disagreed with freeing the slaves.

Key Takeaway 7

The Irish Brigade fought valiantly for the Union in the Civil War.

Analysis

There was much prejudice against the Irish at the time of the Civil War; as a result, many in the Union army and in the public did not believe that Irish troops would serve with distinction and loyalty. There were rumors that Meagher, as brigadier general of the Irish Brigade, was often drunk and a poor commander, in accordance with Irish stereotypes. However, during the war, the Irish Brigade proved itself valiant and determined. The Brigade fought with distinction in numerous battles and stood its ground despite suffering devastating losses at the Battle of Antietam in 1862 and the Battle of Fredericksburg the same year.

Meagher and other Irish who fought for the Union hoped that their display of courage and patriotism would decrease prejudice against them. [13] Black units in the Civil War had similar hopes. Lincoln resisted enlisting black troops because he feared it would alienate border states. But by 1862, white enlistment was decreasing sharply. Eventually 179,000 black soldiers served for the Union. They helped increase popular support for ending slavery and for giving black Americans the right to vote. [14]

The existence of Irish and black units was meant to fight discrimination, but it also demonstrated the power of prejudice. Black and Irish soldiers served in segregated units because commanders were concerned other troops would resent them or refuse to serve with them. The Irish and black units were a sign of progress but also a reminder of ongoing racism.

Key Takeaway 8

The Montana Territory was plagued by vigilante justice. The violence may have led to Meagher's death.

Analysis

Before and during the time Meagher served as acting governor in the Montana Territory, a group of men committed a series of murders in the name of vigilante justice. The vigilantes there were mostly Republicans and Masons. They claimed they were killing thieves who were stealing gold dust. However they often targeted Democrats who supported secession.

When Meagher became acting governor, he was, like many Irish immigrants, sympathetic to the Democrats. This put him in conflict with Republican Wilbur Fisk Sanders, a powerful political figure in the Montana Territory. Shortly before his death, Meagher is reported to have said that he feared for his life. Meagher was killed in a fall from a boat while traveling on the Missouri River. There is some evidence that Sanders may have killed him or may have ordered him killed.

Vigilantism thrived in the Montana Territory in large part because there was not an effective judicial structure. The federal government under Lincoln did not attend closely to setting up a government in the early 1860s. This was understandable, since this was in the middle of the Civil War. The result, however, was a vacuum, in which there was little formal system to prosecute wrongdoers. [15] The same federal neglect caused problems for Meagher as well; he was never able to receive his rightful salary as acting governor, which plunged him into debt. The Wild West was wild because the federal government could not, or did not, assert its authority. Meagher began his life struggling against the overly harsh authoritarian regime of Britain. He ended it struggling with the problems created by absence of government in the Montana Territory.

Author's Style

Timothy Egan's writing is punchy, colorful, and designed to make a vivid impression. He is attentive to language and uses colorful alliterative phrases like "pitiful island prison in the Antipodes." He also includes salacious speculation, hinting that Jane Elgee, or Speranza, may have slept with Meagher while he was imprisoned. He dwells on dramatic and melodramatic details. The book starts with Meagher's fatal plunge into the Missouri River in the Montana Territory, and speculates about whether it was an accident, suicide, or murder.

Meagher lived an exciting life as revolutionary, prisoner, escapee, general, and frontier official, so Egan has a lot of material to work with in crafting a page-turner. Still, at times Egan's style can seem a little too breathless, and the characters a little too flamboyant to be entirely believable. *The Immortal Irishman* presents history as adventure story and Thomas Meagher as a larger-than-life hero, sailing and galloping across the continents. It's entertaining, but at times it can sacrifice balance and accuracy in pursuit of a good yarn.

Author's Perspective

Timothy Egan is a journalist and author well known for his books of popular history. He is not a professional historian or academic. He is, therefore, much more interested in telling a solid, entertaining, interesting narrative than he is in historical debates or in theoretical disputes about historical events.

For example, Egan does not discuss the extent to which historians have been split about the relative importance and value of the Young Ireland movement in which Meagher took part. In fact, Daniel O'Connell, who advocated non-violence, has been more lauded by historians than Meagher and the Young Irelanders. [16] Egan is focused on Meagher, and so Meagher's perspective is foregrounded. O'Connell's refusal to encourage violence is presented in the book as a failure of nerve, rather than as an effort to avoid Irish deaths.

The Immortal Irishman is well-researched and provides a good overview of the breadth of Irish experience in the nineteenth century for the general reader. Those interested in a definitive account of the period, or those who want a better sense of current historical understandings of Ireland, will want to consult other sources as well.

~~~~ END OF INSTAREAD ~~~~

Thank you for purchasing this Instaread book

**Download the Instaread mobile app to get
unlimited text & audio summaries
of bestselling books.**

Visit Instaread.co
to learn more.

References

1. *Economist.* "The Irish famine: opening old wounds." December 12, 2012. Accessed April 6, 2016. http://www.economist.com/blogs/prospero/2012/12/irish-famine

2. Ibid.

3. Rynne, Frank. "Young Ireland and Irish Revolutions." *French Journal of British Studies*, Volume 19, No. 2, 2014, pp. 105-124. Accessed March 22, 2016. https://rfcb.revues.org/265#toctoln10

4. McCartney, Donal. "Young Ireland and the Writing of Irish History review: big men, big ballads, big nation." *Irish Times*, June 20, 2015. Accessed March 22, 2016. http://www.irish-times.com/culture/books/young-ireland-and-the-writing-of-irish-history-review-big-men-big-ballads-big-nation-1.2255914

5. Australian Government. "Convicts and the British colonies in Australia." Accessed March 22, 2016. http://www.australia.gov.au/about-australia/australian-story/convicts-and-the-british-colonies

6. Ibid.

7. Clements, Nicholas. "Tasmania's Black War: a tragic case of lest we remember?" *The Conversation,*

April 24, 2014. Accessed March 23, 2016. http://theconversation.com/tasmanias-black-war-a-tragic-case-of-lest-we-remember-25663

8. Darby, Andrew. "More than 1000 died in Tasmanian war, says historian." *Sydney Morning Herald*, April 28, 2012. Accessed March 23, 2016. http://www.smh.com.au/national/more-than-1000-died-in-tasmanian-war-says-historian-20120427-1xq5p.html

9. Wells, H.G. *The War of the Worlds.* Project Gutenberg. Accessed March 23, 2016. http://www.gutenberg.org/files/36/36-h/36-h.htm

10. Kierdorf, Douglas. "Getting to know the Know-Nothings." *Boston Globe*, January 10, 2016. Accessed March 23, 2016. https://www.boston-globe.com/ideas/2016/01/10/getting-know-know-nothings/yAojakXKkiauKCAzsf4WAL/story.html

11. Ibid.

12. Perry, James DeWolf, and Browne, Katrina. "Civil War's dirty secret about slavery." *CNN*, April 12, 2011. Accessed March 23, 2016. http://www.cnn.com/2011/OPINION/04/12/perry.browne.civil.war/

13. *History Channel*. "The Irish Brigade." Accessed March 24, 2016. http://www.history.com/topics/american-civil-war/the-irish-brigade

14. Freeman, Elsie, Schamel, Wynell Burroughs, and West, Jean. "The Fight for Equal Rights: A Recruiting Poster for Black Soldiers in the Civil War." *Social Education,* Volume 56, Number 2, February 1992, pp. 118-120. [Revised and updated in 1999 by Budge Weidman.] Accessed March 4, 2016. https://www.archives.gov/education/lessons/blacks-civil-war/

15. Ehrlick, Darrell. "New book examines Montana vigilantes through legal lens." *Billings Gazette,* February 2, 2014. Accessed March 24, 2016.

16. http://billingsgazette.com/entertainment/books-and-literature/new-book-examines-montana-vigilantes-through-legal-lens/article_b05b5dc5-3f1d-5478-a03a-4e1f68d3488c.html

17. The Irish Story. "Daniel O'Connell and the Young Irelanders." June 12, 2014. Accessed March 21, 2016. http://www.theirishstory.com/2014/06/12/daniel-oconnell-and-the-young-irelanders/#.VvAv7XChBRk

Lightning Source UK Ltd.
Milton Keynes UK
UKOW06f1120300117
293187UK00001B/34/P